C000203274

CLOSE YOUR EYES

YOU LOOK AT ME

Lauren Pope is a 2019 Manchester Poetry Prize finalist, and winner of the 2021 Brotherton Poetry Prize. Her debut collection, *Always Erase*, was published by Blue Diode Press in 2022. She runs creative writing and literature courses at the Scottish Universities' International Summer School (SUISS) in Edinburgh.

ISBN: 978-1-915079-48-0

Cover designed by Aaron Kent

Edited & Typeset by Aaron Kent

Broken Sleep Books Ltd
Rhydwen
Talgarreg
Ceredigion
SA44 4HB

Broken Sleep Books Ltd
Fair View
St Georges Road
Cornwall
PL26 7YH

Contents

Close your Eyes when you Look at me

Lauren Pope

False Protagonist

In the unforgiving light of
the bread aisle, / I admit I've
asked questions above/ my
councils' leavened wisdom.

Collagen is not a problem /
for bread, is it? More of a
statement, / they sit there
expressionless, beautifully
risen. / Such good listeners.

Mostly, given their proclivity
towards structure, / I ask
about purpose: what
happens to the roots/ of
felled wheat? Do they
remain tangled/ in the
earth's darkness, thirsting?

Bread finds abstraction like
this bewildering. / I tell
them of equal measure:/ a
woman, barely a woman
really, / grown peripheral /
to her own story.

Lush

On a bed of impatiens,
in the orange glow of a security light,
booze dews upon your skin.
How many ripe seedpods would you pinch
if you were conscious?
                    Yes, that old game.

Look at you, shiny,
            oblivious to the ink.

                    Go without your body.
Count ink stains, like sheep:

            a sequin that will not sit properly, 1; the bar door opening, 2;
            the refresh button, 3; the olive's pitted centre – the shape
            of lateness, 4; the refresh button, 5…

                    The bar door opens; the cement, pitted,
                    outside.
                                [refresh]

            Your phone swallowed by the taxi seat, a hungry pit.
                                        sit properly
            The driver's hand on your thigh, hungry.
                                        sit properly
            A pit in your stomach – was it as payment?
                                        sit properly

8

                              [refresh]
                              muffled voices
                              [refresh]
                              their hands
                              [refresh]

The taxi door shutting,
the hungry darkness, a sequin;
and you, like Dorothy amongst
the poppies,
              [refresh]
              your doll eyes opening.

Designs on a Sidewalk

Herringbone
        bent knee
black vein moulding,

horsefly
        exuviae
phlegm marble,
                spew.

Chalk scratch   hop.

PUNK!
        lichen blood,
fungal amadou.

Weed fingerlings
        rise,
        crack through
                alive.

Sadness, too easy a description

1.

I'm circling a feeling,
the act of which is easy to describe:
like a hawk circling prey,
like water circling a drain.
The usual circling metaphors.

The feeling itself, is ineffable, elusive even.
Remember that white albino squirrel
we spotted on the golf course?
Rarer than winning the lottery,
the internet said.
Both incredible
and incredibly disappointing.

We had our phones that day
and didn't even take a photo,
preferring the memory
to the actual image
in case we should discover later
it was really light brown,
or maybe we couldn't be bothered.
That's how memory is - unsure.

2. *taste*

From winter branches
we pull all the days of summer
parcelled into fist-sized suns.

There is a word for this in Portuguese,
tattooed on my sister's neck
like a branding she can't escape, doesn't want to.
It's a secret pet
that needs feeding.

3. *touch*

Two girls clap out:
> *sweet, sweet baby*
> *down by the rollercoaster*

and something reaches out from the vault of me
> *sweet, sweet baby*
> *I'll never let you go*

perhaps an ache to be them again;
I would not choose to go back either.

4. *sight*

Standing on the outside
of a well-lit house
looking in

especially on a cold, dark night –
mist/fog/light drizzle.

It's strange,
remembering something you may not have
personally experienced –
the scene of so many Christmas films.

You did just watch *Home Alone* after all.

5. *sound*

I will describe it by what it's not:
silence
(a common misconception).

Both children will wake
if the house has too much of it.

6. *smell*

Mourning the loss of something
while you still have it,
that place where you give yourself permission
to gently wallow;
the desert after it rains.

Middling: a soliloquy

bullshitfriendlyneighbours   middleagemiddleclass   donotwakethekids
snottysleevesnosnacks   illfittingdresses   weekendsathome
spousalmicroagressions impostersyndrome paychequetopaycheque
deadendcareer   iregrethavingkids   skintagsouvenirs
datenightantithesis   frumpyattire   parentchildmatchingoutfits
currentbehaviourcringespiral   notimeanxiety   thesaggytitshow
midweeksobriety   mykidsknowthepasswordtomyphone

Cleanse

The shallows lap
                    my calves
            with wet tongues.
Could it be that I am the Snow White of water?
            Hear me out, recall
                        the bedlam of woodland creatures
            that played at her feet
                        and what that must have felt like.

I wade in
            (my back / to your face:
            a slow drink).

                        This sweet insignificance,
                        a glass slipper engulfing
                                    my midriff.

Whole and dissolved
in the name of self
            & all that can be imagined –

it is the same reason
I come here.

Those two years: a portrait

start with the hairline, apparently./ treat it as abstraction: a cliff or a coastline/ would be obvious./ a garden border is too, although/ explosions of pampas grass/ like your temper.

so much fuss/ so much meaning attributed/ to the eyes./ paint them as strawberries,/ and think about all the people thinking/ about the meaning of strawberry eyes.

lips move/ practising the act of speaking. colour them/ a cherry red/ because this is the shade you think all grown women wear./ the language you are inhabiting/ is the way you think all grown women speak./ also at this time, you consider the height of glamour to be sips of Diet Coke/ between long drags off a Camel Light for breakfast;/ a lipstick-stained butt.

waves crash out of ears./ that white noise can be felt to this day,/ soothing - like the sounds permeating through the partition wall at night.

you rethink the eyes, acknowledging that strawberries/ were an annoyingly coy thing to do./ they should be black as your sister's first boyfriend's/ – the one who beat her./ paint them as ink stains because she hid it like you grew up in a family of violence;/ because it was so not obvious/ obvious, in hindsight. Your guilt is an ink stain/ for always making this about you.

hell, paint the nose job you wanted;/ paint the smell of orange blossoms in early spring/ as if the whole world lived in the olfactory paradise of your childhood.

remember, angular features (e.g. strong jawline)/ = confidence and manliness (in goodies)/ = aggression and predatory behavior (in baddies)./ this means that, depending on the time of day,/ the portrait can either evoke positive traits (conscientiousness) or negative ones (neuroticism),/ or both simultaneously/ (e.g. an epic display of road rage whilst driving to visit your grandmother).

in the background, different versions of your signature,/ like a form of dress up/ because you had the time/ to endlessly graffiti – on notebooks, on trees and desks,/ on forearms.

there is a photograph of you at 15 looking like a boy/ there is a photograph of you at 17/ looking like a Barbie./ these will make you feel lesser for the rest of your life./ marvel at how, in those two years,/ everything seemed so slow-moving while you waited for your life to begin,/ while you lived your life/ like you were on horseback.

Acknowledgements

The majority of these poems were written over the course of one week in November 2021 while staying at my mother-in-law's house. Thank you, Susan Crombie, for giving us a place to stay while building work was being completed on our house.

Special gratitude goes to the following publications where several of these poems first appeared: *The Glasgow Review of Books* and *Gutter 26*.

Much appreciation to Russell Jones and Marianne MacRae for providing speedy and insightful feedback on the first draft, and to Ross, Garner and Felix for their laughter and support.

Special thanks to Aaron Kent and Broken Sleep for being so kind-hearted, generous, and an absolute delight to work with. You are every poet's dream!

LAY OUT YOUR UNREST

Lightning Source UK Ltd.
Milton Keynes UK
UKHW012015021222
413123UK00006B/361